Ray Palmer

Remember me

The holy communion

Ray Palmer

Remember me
The holy communion

ISBN/EAN: 9783337284039

Printed in Europe, USA, Canada, Australia, Japan

Cover: Foto ©Lupo / pixelio.de

More available books at **www.hansebooks.com**

Remember Me;

OR,

The Holy Communion.

By

RAY PALMER.

Boston:
THE AMERICAN TRACT SOCIETY.

Depositories, 28 Cornhill, Boston; and 13 Bible House,
Astor Place. New York.

TO THE

MEMBERS OF THE CHURCH TO WHICH HE MINISTERS,

ESPECIALLY TO

The Younger Members,

IN WHOSE UNION TO CHRIST HE GREATLY REJOICES, AND FOR WHOSE CHRISTIAN GROWTH AND COMFORT HE HABITUALLY PRAYS,

THIS LITTLE VOLUME IS INSCRIBED

BY THEIR AFFECTIONATE FRIEND AND PASTOR,

RAY PALMER.

PREFACE.

To young disciples, it is a question of deep and serious interest with what specific thoughts and spiritual affections the table of the Lord should be approached. In the case of older Christians, likewise, great care should be taken that the inward exercises connected with the occasion should be such as are demanded by the nature and design of this most precious ordinance. To both classes it is hoped that this little volume may be useful.

It will be seen that these pages are intended to speak *directly to the heart*. It is sought to bring the great facts pertaining to Christ's work of redeeming by his death, which are set forth in the ordinance of the Holy Supper, into immediate contact with the religious sensibilities.

Preface.

The plan of the volume will explain itself. Prose and poetry are intermingled, for the sake of variety, and as speaking to the heart in different ways. The poetical pieces, most of them, have been written for the place they occupy. The hymns, "Jesus, these eyes have never seen," "O Bread to pilgrims given!" and "Jesus, thou Joy of loving hearts," were contributed to the Sabbath Hymn Book, to the proprietors of which they now belong. They are used here by permission. "My faith looks up to thee," although so familiar, is inserted at the end, because it seemed to form so fitting a conclusion to the book.

R. P.

Contents.

INVOCATION	9
TEXTS ON THE INSTITUTION OF THE LORD'S SUPPER	10
DESIGN OF THE ORDINANCE	12
QUESTIONS FOR SELF-EXAMINATION	15
HYMN: CHRIST LOVED UNSEEN	18
FIRST MEDITATION: ANTICIPATION. — Monday Evening	21
SONNET: THE ANOINTING	26
STANZAS: "I SAW THEE"	27
SECOND MEDITATION: THE PASSOVER. — Tuesday Evening	29
SONNET: THE ALARM	36
HYMN: SELF-DEVOTION	37
THIRD MEDITATION: THE UNMASKING. — Wednesday Evening	39
SONNET: THE DEPARTURE	45
STANZAS: SELF-SEARCHING	46
FOURTH MEDITATION: THE HOLY SUPPER. — Thursday Even'g	49
SONNET: THE INSTITUTION	56
SACRAMENTAL HYMN	57
FIFTH MEDITATION: PARTING WORDS. — Friday Evening	59

Contents.

SONNET: THE HOLY BOND	66
STANZAS: THE UNITY OF LOVE .	67
SIXTH MEDITATION: GETHSEMANE.—Saturday Evening .	69
SONNET: GETHSEMANE . .	76
STANZAS: "IN THE GARDEN WITH HIM"	77
SEVENTH MEDITATION: CALVARY.—Sabbath Morning	79
SONNET: THE SACRIFICE . .	86
STANZAS: VIA DOLOROSA .	87
AT THE TABLE	89
AFTER THE SACRAMENT.—Sabbath Evening .	96
HYMN: DELIGHT IN CHRIST . . .	99
HYMN: FAITH	101

REMEMBER ME.

INVOCATION.

BLESSED Lord Jesus! I recognize the sacrament of the Holy Supper as instituted by thee for the refreshment and comfort of truly renewed and believing souls, and as designed to be a perpetual ordinance in thy visible Church. I would be prepared to keep this sacred feast in obedience to thy command. May the Holy Spirit graciously assist and guide me! Amen.

THE INSTITUTION.

Matt. 26 : 26-30.

JESUS took bread, and blessed *it*, and brake *it*, and gave *it* to the disciples, and said, Take, eat; this is my body. And he took the cup, and gave thanks, and gave *it* to them, saying, Drink ye all of it; for this is my blood of the new testament, which is shed for many for the remission of sins. But I say unto you, I will not drink henceforth of this fruit of the vine, until that day when I drink it new with you in my Father's kingdom.

And, when they had sung a hymn, they went out into the Mount of Olives.

The Institution.

1 Cor. 11 : 23-25.

For I have received of the Lord that which also I delivered unto you, That the Lord Jesus, the same night in which he was betrayed, took bread: and, when he had given thanks, he brake *it*, and said, Take, eat; this is my body, which is broken for you: this do in remembrance of me. After the same manner also *he took* the cup, when he had supped, saying, This cup is the new testament in my blood: this do ye, as oft as ye drink *it*, in remembrance of me.

DESIGN OF THE ORDINANCE.

THE sacrament of the Holy Supper was plainly instituted *for Christ's disciples.* None else could possibly enter into the spirit of the observance. Only love can find pleasure in communion with Christ, and in dwelling with deliberate and protracted meditation on the scenes connected with his sufferings and death. It was meant to be a *distinguishing* ordinance, separating those who should observe it from the irreligious world, and marking them as avowed followers of Jesus.

For whom designed.

A mark of discipleship.

2. It was further intended to be at once the symbol of a truth, and the seal or confirmation of a covenant. By its observance, the great essential truth of the Christian atonement was to be visibly acknowledged and kept fresh in the heart of the Church, and to be set forth in the sight of all the world. By receiving it, each believer most solemnly covenants with his Lord to love and serve him, and renews the pledge as often as he repeats his attendance at the table.

Intended as a symbol and a seal.

3. The Holy Supper was also designed to convey to each participant who should rightly receive it divine nourishment, spiritual life and health and joy, the quickening of right desires, and the confirming of the purpose of faithful Christian living. This through the inward ap-

To convey divine life and comfort.

prehension of Christ, and the appropriation of his grace by faith.

4. Finally, Christ wished, by the sacrament of the Supper, to unite those who loved him into an intimate fellowship, or brotherhood, cemented by mutual sympathy and affection; and so to make the many members feel themselves to be but one body in him.

<small>To secure the unity of believers.</small>

SELF-EXAMINATION.

HAVE I truly and deeply felt that I was by nature estranged from God and goodness,— was one of the *lost* whom Jesus came to save?

2. Have I reason, in the consciousness of what I feel, for a comfortable hope that my heart has been renewed by the Holy Spirit, and that I have truly received Christ by faith?

3. Is it my sincere desire, and steadfast purpose, and daily resolute endeavor, to deny and subdue myself, to put on the Christian graces, and to grow in likeness of Christ?

4. Do I habitually remember, and strive

faithfully to keep, the promises made in my public profession of religion?

5. Do I depend alone on Christ's atoning sacrifice for pardon and peace with God, and on his power to keep me unto everlasting life?

6. Am I consciously prepared lovingly and gratefully to give myself anew to Christ my Lord while I sit with him at his table, and to renew in all sincerity my covenant-vows?

REMARKS.
It will serve but little purpose merely to read the preceding questions over. If you will profit by them, reader, take them up one by one; interrogate most seriously and faithfully your heart; and after deliberate reflection, as in the sight of God, who searches the secret soul, answer truly

SELF-EXAMINATION.

to yourself. You will not be likely to find either comfort or strength in coming to the Saviour's table, unless you can honestly answer these questions, with a good degree of confidence, in the affirmative. Remember the words of the apostle: "Let a man examine himself, and so let him eat of this bread, and drink of this cup."

PRAYER.

O Thou who knowest my inmost heart! help me in all sincerity to answer these questions to myself and to thee, as in thy most holy presence; and dispose my heart aright, that I may profitably meet thee at thy board; through Jesus Christ my Lord. Amen.

CHRIST LOVED UNSEEN.

ESUS, these eyes have never seen
    That radiant form of thine!
The vail of sense hangs dark between
    Thy blessed face and mine!

I see thee not, I hear thee not;
    Yet art thou oft with me;
And earth hath ne'er so dear a spot
    As where I meet with thee.

Like some bright dream, that comes unsought,
    When slumbers o'er me roll,
Thine image ever fills my thought,
    And charms my ravished soul.

Yet though I have not seen, and still
    Must rest in faith alone,
I love thee, dearest Lord! and will, —-
    Unseen, but not unknown

When death these mortal eyes shall seal,
    And still this throbbing heart,
The rending vail shall thee reveal,
    All glorious as thou art.

PREPARATORY EXERCISES.

I. ANTICIPATION.

MONDAY EVENING.

AGAIN the day approaches when I may keep the Christian feast of holy love. Delightful occasion! I welcome its return. Do *this* — this simple but most expressive act — in remembrance of ME! Yes, Lord! with solemn joy I will. The command is full of wisdom and of grace. The sacrament so instituted in thy

Joyful anticipation of the sacrament.

Luke 22: 19.

Church is at once divinely touching, and admirably adapted to the necessities of thy disciples. I recognize in it a special call to self-examination, and to a renewed withdrawing of my affections from their too eager pursuit of inferior good. Each day, therefore, until the season comes, I will set apart an hour — it shall be, as now, the peaceful evening hour, if possible — in which, withdrawn from the noisy world, I may commune with my own heart, and meditate on Christ's great sacrifice. Come, Jesus, and bless these moments with thy presence.

<small>*The evening hour.*</small>

I sit in this quiet hour, and look at the fading west. The sun has disappeared. But see what glory he still sheds upon the world! Though himself no longer seen, his beams still bathe woods, fields, and streams, and yonder float-

<small>*Christ the Light of the soul.*</small>

ANTICIPATION.   23

ing clouds, in rosy light. Even so my blessed Lord, the Sun of righteousness,— though no more for a season visible to mortal eyes, — sheds a sweet radiance on his Church, a soft and twilight radiance, grateful to loving souls; and, like the evening light of polar regions, not fading till the morning breaks again, and he re-appears. Though now I see him not, yet, believing, I am cheered ever with somewhat of his light, the reflection of which is the beauty of all saints. Rejoice in him, my soul! *Christ cheers his own till he comes again.*

At the sacramental table I may meet him, if my heart is ready to receive so divine a guest. Contact with the world begets a sense of defilement, even where there is no consciousness of deliberate willful sin; and it is good *Christ comes to the prepared heart.*

to return to the fountain, and wash and be clean. When the cares and the business of life have hurried me hither and thither with no little distraction of mind, I love to come back again, and sit down before the cross, and gaze on the blessed Sufferer with silent, tender memories. I love to devote myself to him anew, and to repeat the vows made in the days of my espousals. It is like coming once more into the sunshine after long walking through gloom and mist. Let me come to thy table, Lord, with right affections and with a lively faith, that I lose not the benefits of the occasion. To a heart not graciously prepared, there is nothing life-giving even in the sight of the cross, and of the divine Victim offered there. Grant me then, O Jesus! beforehand, such

Self-consecration renewed.

1 Cor. 11: 28, 29.
No profit to a careless heart.

self-abasement for sin, such rekindling of faith and hope, and such discoveries of the fullness of thy grace and love, that I may find new life and joy while with thy people I shall sit and commune with thee. Hast thou not said, "He that loveth me shall be loved of my Father, and I will love him, and will manifest myself unto him"? Come, then, and give me to feel most consciously that thou art with me here. Blessed then, indeed, shall the moments be! Awake, O north wind! and come, thou south! blow upon my garden, that the spices thereof may flow out. From my soul, warmed by the breath of the Spirit, may the fragrant perfume of holy affection ascend to Christ! Then let my Beloved come into his garden, and eat his pleasant fruits.

John 14: 21.

Christ's presence invited.

Sol. Song 4:16.

THE ANOINTING.

Mark 13 : 3-9.

SHE came — the sinful — while he brake
    the bread,
Her broken heart now healed, and brim-
    ming o'er
With holy burning love; she came to pour
Sweet, precious odors on that reverend head;
And — as by deep, prophetic impulse led —
That sacred body, soon uplifted high
'Mid scorn and shame, in agony to die,
Betimes to anoint for its sepulchral bed.
Ungrudgingly she did the loving deed;
For to that glowing heart no offering seemed
Too rich for Him, no cost too dear she deemed,
If he with one kind look the gift might heed.
The selfish chid; pronounced her act a crime:
He praised, and bade it live to latest time!

I SAW THEE.

When thou wast under the fig-tree, I saw thee.—John 1 : 48.

I SAW thee when, as twilight fell,
    And Evening lit her fairest star,
    Thy footsteps sought yon quiet dell,
    The world's confusion left afar.

I saw thee when thou stood'st alone
    Where drooping branches thick o'erhung—
Thy still retreat to all unknown—
    Hid in deep shadows darkly flung.

I saw thee, when, as died each sound
    Of bleating flocks or woodland bird,
Kneeling, as if on holy ground,
    Thy voice the listening silence heard.

I saw thy calm uplifted eyes,
    And marked the heaving of thy breast,
When rose to heaven thy heartfelt sighs ·
    For purer life, for perfect rest.

I saw the light that o'er thy face
　　Stole with a soft suffusing glow,
As if, within, celestial grace
　　Breathed the same bliss that angels know.

I saw — what thou didst not — above
　　Thy lowly head an open heaven;
And tokens of thy Father's love,
　　With smiles, to thy rapt spirit given.

I saw thee from that sacred spot
　　With firm and peaceful soul depart;
I, Jesus, saw thee, — doubt it not, —
　　And read the secrets of thy heart!

II. THE PASSOVER.

TUESDAY EVENING.

IRST in the series of events immediately connected with the Redeemer's death was the last passover. In the endeavor to prepare my soul for the sacramental communion of his great sacrifice, let me begin at this point, and attend him through some of the painful scenes that followed.

Evening of the Passover.

He sat down with the twelve. How simple is the statement! and yet how much does it express! His hour, as he knew, was just at hand. He must needs

Matthew 26 : 20.

perform now his last acts, and make himself ready to be offered. Once more he will keep that great national feast in which his own death, as the true paschal lamb, was represented. How full of meaning it must always have been to him! But this was to be his *last* observance of it before the shedding of his own availing blood upon the cross. The type was now to be fulfilled in that great sacrifice, in view of which the angel of wrath should *pass over* the true Israel, and spare them as redeemed from death. There was every thing in the occasion to move his heart profoundly. He was immediately to part from his beloved disciples: worse still, he was to be himself deliberately forsaken by them for a season, and to tread the winepress alone. All this was in his thought. Yet what sublime collectedness of

It is the last feast.

The Passover.

soul! No perturbation, no appeal for sympathy or comfort, no want of his usual perfect equanimity. He exhibits his wonted calmness, mingled with dignity and sweetness; was, in a word, altogether like himself. Dear Lord! what steadiness of purpose, what devotion to thy work, and what strength of holy love, were thine! Help me herein more faithfully to copy thee. For lack of these thy graces, thy chosen friends were overcome by the fear of man, and failed in the hour of trial. Let me not weakly falter, if for thy sake, and in the way of duty, I am brought to face suffering and shame.

Jesus divinely calm.

Let me admire, too, the compassion and tenderness of Jesus in these affecting circumstances. When the disciples, not yet understanding the nature of his kingdom, and ignorant of the

Ambition of the disciples.

future, disputed, in a selfish and ambitious spirit, which of them should be greatest, he mildly taught them that no such questions should ever be raised among his servants. Then, to enforce his teachings by his personal example, he himself assumed the office of a servant, and with his own hands washed and wiped their feet! How touching, and yet how pungent, the rebuke implied! How memorable are the words of comment which he added!—"If I, then, your Lord and Master, have washed your feet, ye ought also to wash one another's feet." It was thus that he taught his followers in all time to be clothed with humility, and to cultivate and exhibit a spirit of mutual helpfulness and love. Ah, Lord! how few of us have

Luke 22 : 24-27.

Christ washes their feet.

John 13 : 14.

The lesson of humility and love.

The Passover.

thoroughly learned this lesson! But too little care for each other is seen among those who bear thy name. Comparatively few are ready to perform for each other self-denying services, or even the little acts of kindness to which love naturally prompts. Have I not myself been greatly deficient in Christ-like care and affection for my brethren? Have I not failed especially to condescend to them that are of low estate, and to seek their good? Forgive, O Holy One! my self-seeking, uncharitableness, and pride. Assist me to love all thine for thy dear sake, and kindly to minister even to the humblest, as opportunity may offer. *Self-scrutiny.*

Ye are not all clean! No: fearful words! In the little band of cherished friends, there was one false, hollow-hearted traitor. Perhaps not, *John 13:11. The betrayal announced.*

in the beginning, consciously a hypocrite. Quite probably he had been self-deceived, and had believed himself a true disciple; yet all the while his Lord had recognized in him a devil. Dear Lord! and is this possible? May I, though I have thought I loved thee, though I have borne thy blessed name and have sat around thy table, be counted of thee an enemy even now, and fall away from thee at length? When sometimes my heart grows languid in its devotion, remiss in its watchfulness, and engrossed with earthly interests; when the remembrances of thy cross and passion are infrequent, or seem in a measure to have lost their power to move me to grateful tenderness, — I tremble lest my hold on thee should fail entirely, and should prove to be something less than the unyielding grasp of

John 6:70.

Salutary fear.

a true and living faith. Yet I can not endure to think of this. How but in thee can my soul, that longs for sympathy, for rest, for purity, be satisfied? Disowned of thee, what would remain for me but a hopeless wretchedness like that of the false apostle? "Search me, O God! and know my heart; try me, and know my thoughts; and see if there be any wicked way in me, and lead me in the way everlasting." *Psalm 139: 23, 24.*

THE ALARM.

HE kept the Passover; it was his last:
   For now drew near the great predestined day
   When of man's mighty guilt himself should pay,
With dying groans, and blood, the ransom vast.
The cross was in his eye; the hours flew fast:
Yet calm he sat, and looked serenely round
On all the twelve; while they, with awe profound,
And loving gaze on him, revolved the past,
The future from them hid: then, touched, he said,
"Of you, one shall betray me unto death!"
At that dire word, BETRAY, they all did start,
As if a thunder-peal had stilled each breath,
Or sudden mortal pang shot through each heart:
"Lord! is it I?" each cried with horrid dread.

SELF-DEVOTION.

TAKE me, O my Father! take me,
    Take me, save me through thy Son;
That which thou wouldst have me, make me:
    Let thy will in me be done.

Long from thee my footsteps straying,
    Thorny proved the way I trod:
Weary come I now, and praying;
    Take me to thy love, my God.

Fruitless years with grief recalling,
    Humbly I confess my sin;
At thy feet, O Father! falling:
    To thy household take me in.

Freely now to thee I proffer
    This relenting heart of mine;
Freely life and soul I offer,—
    Gift unworthy love like thine!

Once the world's Redeemer, dying,
   Bare our sins upon the tree:
On that sacrifice relying,
   Now I look in hope to thee.

Father, take me; all forgiving,
   Fold me to thy loving breast:
In thy love for ever living,
   I must be for ever blest.

III. THE UNMASKING.

WEDNESDAY EVENING.

UDAS, though he had flattered himself that the baseness of his heart was yet unknown to Christ, must have been undeceived by those few and quiet words — "Thou hast said. That thou doest do quickly." He withdrew at once from a presence he could no longer bear. Conscious guilt must needs desire to escape the presence of spotless purity. Fixed in his wicked purpose, his own conscience compelled the traitor to separate himself for ever

The traitor exposed.

Matt. 26: 25. John 13: 27.

from the loving and true-hearted disciples, and from the holy Jesus. From that hour he became an outcast. "He went out, and it was night," says the evangelist; night not only around him, but yet more dismal night within his soul. He departed from that company of the faithful, because he was never of them, and not because a real tie of love between himself and Christ had now been broken. So, soon or late, will every deceived or consciously false heart reveal itself. At the bar of judgment, if not sooner, Christ will strip off all disguises, and exhibit every character precisely as it is. O Saviour! let me not then be found to have been either a deliberate hypocrite, or blindly self-deluded.

He departs finally from Christ.

1 John 2: 19.

A wrong heart sure to be revealed.

The departure of Judas must have been a

The Unmasking. 41

relief to the blessed Jesus. Now he could speak freely to those, who, in spite of their weakness of faith and their defects, were all of them truly his. *The withdrawing of Judas a relief to Jesus* He alluded in plain terms to the approaching end of his earthly mission, and to his departure from the world to enter into his glorified estate. *John 13: 31-33.* Yet he withheld much; for he would spare their feelings. Having loved his own which were in the world, *he loved them to the end;* *John 13: 1.* and he could freely give expression to his affection. Happy eleven! what can be so delightful as to be allowed, in the character of confidential friends, to enjoy, apart from the world, free intercourse with Christ? *Blessed to be with Christ.* This, Lord, thou givest all who truly love thee leave to do at the sacramental table. With thine, and near to thee, do I earnestly desire to sit, whoever may withdraw. Methinks I hear thee ask, "Wilt thou also go away?" and my heart answers, "Lord, to whom shall I go? Thou hast the words of eternal life." No, no, my blessed Master! As thou shalt keep me, I will never depart from thee, never neglect to meet thee with thine own around thy sacred board.

<small>John 6:67, 68.</small>

And wilt thou not help me, that, weak as in myself I am, I may cleave to thee without faltering? "I know my sheep, and am known of mine. I give unto them eternal life, and they shall never perish, neither shall any pluck them out of my hands." Such are thy precious words. On these I may rely. The great, decisive question is, Am I indeed acknowledged of thee as

<small>Jesus will help his own.</small>

<small>John 10: 14, 28.</small>

<small>The momentous question.</small>

The Unmasking.

thine? Judas was counted in thine household; but thou didst see in him a son of perdition all the while. My heart, in all its secret recesses, is thoroughly known to thee. Dost thou discern in me even a little faith and love? Again and again I ask myself if I am truly joined to thee. As often as I prepare to meet thee in the Holy Supper, the inquiry suggests itself anew; and far as I am from complete conformity to thee, when I listen to the response from my inmost heart, it *does* seem to testify that I bear thee a true affection. I do feel at times — unless I am totally deceived — a delightful consciousness that the Spirit beareth witness with my spirit that I am a child of God. When thou sayest to my soul, "Lovest thou me?" I do seem able to appeal to thee to answer for

_{The inward witness of the Spirit. Rom. 8:16.}

me — able to say with Peter, "Lord, thou knowest all things; thou *knowest* that I love thee." Dear Lord, confirm my faith and hope. Give me a sweeter assurance of thy love than ever I have had before at this approaching feast; while the recollection of the fall of Judas fills me with a salutary fear. Separation from thee and thine! I can not endure the thought.

John 21:15.

THE DEPARTURE.

HE loved disciple lay upon his breast,
    Drinking sweet influence from that voice
        divine:
    He asked; the Master gave at once the
        sign
That marked the traitor, justified the rest.
Then with convicting glance, while yet dismay
Sat on the faces of the innocent,
He said — and Judas knew the deep intent —
"What thou hast purposed, DO without delay."
Heart-smitten, out into the murky night
Went he, foul demons ruling all his soul,
And floods of hate that surged without control:
Then Jesus cried — his eyes beamed heavenly
    light —
"Now shall the Son of man — betrayed, denied —
Before all men, by God be glorified!"

SELF-SEARCHING.

OH, tell me, Jesus! to my heart—
    My troubled heart — the secret tell;
May I from thee and thine depart,
    As Judas when he falsely fell?
    Is it not love, this kindling flame
That warms my breast oft as thy name
    Falls on my willing ear?
Is it not faith that oft hath brought
My trembling soul the peace it sought,
    And stilled each restless fear?

This quiet joy that hidden flows
    Deep in my soul; that makes me glad,
Though many a rude wind round me blows,
    And many a sorrow makes me sad —
Can this calm joy, that ever lives,
Be aught but that thy presence gives,

SELF-SEARCHING.

To faithful souls revealed —
The presence and the loving smile
That gladden all thine own — the while
From unbelief concealed?

The tears that oft these eyes have wept
When I before thy feet have knelt,
Or watch about thy cross have kept,
And all thy pangs have keenly felt —
Came they not from that holy grief
That brings the broken heart relief,
And softens it to love?
Was not the hope that wakened there
Hope that shall triumph o'er despair,
And bear the soul above?

Speak, thou that knowest well — decide;
If I am thine, oh! clasp this hand;
And when my feet would stray or slide,
Then firmly hold and bid me stand.

Go forth from thee? Give me to bear
Thy bitter cross, thy thorns to wear;
 But let me not depart!
No, Lord: afresh to thee I bring
A free, a cheerful offering,—
 This trusting, grateful heart.

IV. THE HOLY SUPPER.

THURSDAY EVENING.

HRIST and his disciples had now finished the Passover. The great event typified by the paschal lamb — the slaying of the appointed Lamb of God, who should take away the sin of the world — was just at hand. *Christ our Passover. 1 Cor. 5 : 7.* The Lord, before he would be offered up, would set every thing in order, with a careful foresight of the future needs of his disciples. The time had come, therefore, for the institution of an ordinance, which, to the end of time, might serve at once to express and

to sustain the faith of those who should believe.

It was the design of the blessed Jesus that his kingdom in the world should take a visible form; that is to say, that his disciples, by some appropriate act and testimony, should become known to each other and to the unbelieving world as his. It was his purpose, also, that they should have fellowship one with another, and that they all, by a living faith and a holy sympathy, should be united to him, their Saviour and their life, and should perpetually confirm their souls by cherishing and keeping fresh the memory of his sacrificial death. Who but himself would ever have thought of accomplishing this end by means so very simple?

<small>Christ will have a visible Church. Matt. 10: 32. Mark 16: 16.</small>

<small>John 17: 20, 21.</small>

Collect thyself, then, O my soul! and

behold thy Lord while he institutes, to be observed throughout all time, this touching Christian sacrament — the taking of consecrated bread and wine as memorials of him. Listen while with words of prayer he sets apart these very familiar elements to a high and holy use. Then hear him say to the wondering disciples not yet prepared to understand him, "Take, eat; this is my body which is broken for you: this do in remembrance of me." And again, taking the cup with thanksgiving, "This is my blood of the new testament, which is shed for many for the remission of sins: this do ye, as oft as ye drink it, in remembrance of me." It is a truly divine simplicity with which the Master thus sets forth, for the instruction and com-

The thoughts fixed on the institution.

Matt. 26: 26-29.

Luke 22: 19-20.

A memorial rite, and beautifully simple.

fort of all believers, the momentous spiritual truths involved in his cross and passion.

The act of eating and drinking with one, from ancient times, and especially among Oriental nations, has been significant of mutual confidence and affection, and a pledge of perpetual friendship. By it the Saviour means, that, in the sacramental feast, his followers shall at once acknowledge and pledge anew, from time to time, their love to one another and to him. But he goes still farther. He anticipates, what from them was yet concealed, that he should be to the world the Lamb slain, — the true Paschal Lamb, — at the sight of which, Eternal Justice should *pass over* the sins of the penitent and believing. He knows that he is soon to bear upon his head, and in his hands

The act of eating and drinking with one a pledge of friendship.

Christ the true Paschal Lamb.

and feet and pierced side, the marks of agonies endured on behalf of guilty man. Broken for you! Yes, dearest Lord! thou wast wounded for *our* transgressions; thou wast bruised for *our* iniquities. Thou didst bear our sins in thine own body on the tree.

_{Isa. 53:5.}
_{1 Pe. 2:24.}

> "'Twas for my sins my dearest Lord
> Hung on the accursed tree;
> And groaned away a dying life
> For thee, my soul, for thee!"

I see in this bread thy lacerated, suffering body, and through thy sacred wounds I penetrate to the anguish of thy spirit. This cup, to me, is the fit symbol of thy blood — the blood of the great atonement — shed for the remission of sin. As I look upon

The Supper the symbol of Christ's sufferings and of his atoning death.

this wine, I remember that without the shedding of blood there could be no remission, and that thou, by thine own blood, hast entered in once into the holy place, having obtained eternal redemption for me, a sinful soul — for all who rest on thy once-offered sacrifice.

<small>Heb. 9:22.</small>

<small>Heb. 9:12.</small>

Yes, thou that takest away the sin of the world, eating this bread and drinking this cup, thy disciples shall show forth thy death until thou come. So will we tell the world and each other that we are thine. When, with my fellow-Christians, I shall again observe thy sacramental ordinance, I will tenderly and thankfully remember thee, thy painful and bloody death. I will lay my soul once more beneath thy cross; will repeat with hearty joy the vows of faithful love and ser-

<small>The observance of the Supper a testimony to the world.</small>

vice: and by faith my soul shall feast on thee the Bread of life, and drink of thee the spiritual Rock, asking for nothing more than out of thy fullness to be richly and perpetually filled. Prepare thou me to meet thee at thy table. Let thy cup of blessing which is blessed be indeed to me the communion of thy blood; and the bread which is broken, the communion of thy body.

<small>Christ spiritually received in the sacrament.</small>

<small>1 Cor. 10: 16.</small>

THE INSTITUTION.

HE took the bread, and blessed it. Then he brake,
And gave to each, and said — oh words sublime ! —
"This is my body broken ! Through all time,
In memory of my death, this emblem take."
Next for the cup gave thanks. For his dear sake,
He bade them taste the wine. "Drink: 'tis my blood,
The seal and witness of all grace in God,
Till when the judgment trump the dead shall wake."
Oh sacred mystery ! communion sweet
Of holy, loving souls, in which they flow
All into one blest brotherhood, and meet
Ineffably their Lord, and joy to know
That at this simple board they feast with Him
Whose face unveiled fires the rapt seraphim !

SACRAMENTAL HYMN.

O BREAD to pilgrims given!
    O Food that angels eat!
    O Manna sent from heaven,
        For heaven-born natures meet!
    Give us, for thee long pining,
To eat till richly filled;
Till, earth's delights resigning,
    Our every wish is stilled!

O Water, life-bestowing,
    From out the Saviour's heart!
A Fountain purely flowing,
    A Fount of love, thou art.
Oh, let us, freely tasting,
    Our burning thirst assuage!
Thy sweetness, never wasting,
    Avails from age to age.

Jesus, this feast receiving,
  We thee, unseen, adore;
Thy faithful word believing,
  We take, and doubt no more.
Give us, thou true and loving,
  On earth to live in thee;
Then, death the vail removing,
  Thy glorious face to see!

Translated from Thomas Aquinas.

V. PARTING WORDS.

FRIDAY EVENING.

OUR Lord and his chosen friends seem to have lingered a while around the table, after the institution of the Supper; while he, mindful of their approaching trials, so immediately connected with his own, discoursed to them at length. He spoke as knowing himself the future, but without lifting the vail to disclose it fully to their view. When he had reached the point at which the fourteenth chapter of John closes, they appear to have risen from the table, as

The Saviour discourses after the Supper.

if with the purpose of departing.

<small>John 14: 31.</small>

But probably, as they stood grouped together after rising, the conversation recommenced, and the Saviour went on again, as recorded in the fifteenth and sixteenth chapters; and then concluded the interview with prayer. This supposition agrees with all the circumstances, and is much more probable than that this delightful conversation occurred out of doors as they were walking. The whole spirit of the words addressed to the disciples, and of the sublime prayer that followed, savors of retirement — of a secluded, quiet place — and would ill befit the wayside.

<small>The conversation and prayer not out of doors.</small>

Parting words! They are always affecting, the more in proportion as the person uttering them is venerated and beloved. The last words of a father or a mother or an honored and cherished friend, when about to leave the world, are wont to be kept by the survivors as the jewels of the heart. But while, as his parting words, these last sayings of the Lord Jesus have a deep and peculiar interest, they are yet more precious because of the invaluable truths and promises which they embody. They furnish a solid ground for faith to rest upon amidst all trials and throughout all time. They breathe the deepest tenderness, the purest love, and the most divine tranquillity of soul. In these words, the whole Church of the redeemed, down to the last day of the world, have an individual concern. They belong to me personally, if I am Christ's. While now once more I read and meditate upon them, may

The words of Jesus touching, because the last before he suffered.

They are rich in truth and comfort.

He spoke to believers in all time.

they come warm and fresh to my soul, as if from the lips of my blessed Master!

And most naturally do they connect themselves with the sacramental season, in that I am to commemorate my Saviour's death for me, and these are his words of comfort spoken for me as he went to die. How like him was it to be then chiefly occupied, not with his own coming anguish, but with the trials awaiting those who should be left without him amidst an evil and hostile world! Let me emulate this forgetfulness of self. Let me be more intent on ministering strength and sympathy to others than on moving them to pity by recounting my own distresses. Forget not, O my soul, in what spirit thy Saviour spoke when the hour of his own great sorrows was even now at hand.

John 16: 13.

Like Christ, to be most mindful of others.

Let not YOUR *heart be troubled!* This is the key-note of his wonderful discourse. _{John 14:1.}

Ah, dearest Lord, how hard is this for our weak faith! How difficult to confide in thee, and fear nothing! Yet why should I be anxious? Of what should I be afraid? In that covenant, which at thy table I am going to renew again as I have done so often, every thing absolutely which is involved in my perfect safety and my best well-being thou hast bound thyself to give me. A mansion in thy Father's house; the promise that thou thyself wilt come and bring me to it — wilt send the Comforter with a ministry even better to me than thine — wilt thyself come and make thine abode with me — wilt permit me to live in thee as

_{Faith must be strong to conquer fear.}

_{John 14: 2, 3.}

_{John 16:7.}

_{John 14: 23.}

the branch liveth in the vine; and then the unqualified permission to ask and receive till my joy shall be full — such are the gifts of thy most faithful love. Well didst thou say, "Not as the world giveth give I unto thee."

<small>John 15: 1-5.
John 15: 11.
John 14: 27.</small>

O blessed Jesus! assist me, while I sit with thee at thy table, with warm affection and unhesitating confidence to intrust myself, in body and soul, for life and death, to thee. Help thou me also, after thy divine example, to feel a generous love and a tender care for my fellow-disciples, and to go out of myself in ministering, as opportunity is given, to their encouragement and comfort. Thou hast said, "This is my commandment, *That ye love one another* as I have loved you." Do thou enable me to re-

<small>Prayer for faith and love.

Mutual love commanded.
John 13: 34.</small>

member this as a portion of thy parting charge, and to count even the humblest of thy followers my brother, or sister, well beloved for thy dear sake. Let me not forget that these are to be my companions and the sharers of my joy in the world above, and that thou acknowledgest every act of kindness done to them as if done unto thyself. By patience with all their infirmities and faults, and tender sympathy with their burdens and their sorrows, let me be prepared to hear thee say to me at last, "Inasmuch as thou hast done it unto the least of these my brethren, thou hast done it unto Me." *Matt. 25: 40.*

THE HOLY BOND.

A LITTLE while, he said, and hence I go;
  And ye shall seek me, but ye shall not
      find:
Ye may not follow now; but left behind,
  My witnesses, the world by you shall know
The truth; that truth strike root, and grow;
A holy kingdom rise, and wide extend,
Till e'en earth's proudest shall submissive bend,
And unto me all tribes and nations flow.
Behold, a new command to you I give —
Love one another: all who will be mine
Let love in one blest fellowship combine,
That each for all, and all for each, may live.
So, marked of men, shall ye, 'mid earth's dim night,
Divinely glow with pure celestial light.

THE UNITY OF LOVE.

LORD, thou on earth didst love thine own—
    Didst love them to the end:
Oh! still, from thy celestial throne,
    Let gifts of love descend.

The love the Father bears to thee,
    His own eternal Son,
Fill all thy saints, till all shall be
    In pure affection one.

As thou for us didst stoop so low,
    Warmed by Love's holy flame,
So let our deeds of kindness flow
    To all who bear thy name.

One blessed fellowship in love,
    Thy living Church should stand,
Till, faultless, she at last above
    Shall shine at thy right hand.

Oh glorious day, when she, the Bride,
    With her dear Lord appears;
When, robed in beauty at his side,
    She shall forget her tears!

VI. GETHSEMANE.

SATURDAY EVENING.

WHEN our Lord had ended the memorable conversation and prayer which followed the institution of the sacrament of the Supper, he went forth, attended by his disciples, to Gethsemane. Of the twelve, he here selected three — Peter, James, and John — and took them with him to a little distance from the rest. Then, reminding these of their need of watchfulness and prayer, he separated himself even from them,

<small>He goeth to the Garden of Gethsemane. John 18:1.</small>

<small>Matt. 26: 36, 37, 41.</small>

and went still farther, that he might be alone. There it was that the most affecting scene in all his life, save only that of Calvary, occurred.

The hour had come in which it was permitted to the powers of darkness and to his malicious enemies to do their worst against the holy Jesus. He knew all that was before him. He had clear foresight not only of the outward and merely natural suffering through which he was immediately to pass, but also of those inward and supernatural distresses which were involved in his work of expiation, and which must needs be, in a great measure, incomprehensible to us. His humanity was not a mere appearance: it was real and complete. As a man, he had lived a life conformed entirely to the ordinary

John 22: 53. He knows that his hour of suffering has come.

human conditions. He exhibited the common sensibilities of our nature. He suffered, being tempted. It is not wonderful, therefore, that in the near prospect of his last great conflict, all the details of which he perfectly well knew, he should have been exceedingly sorrowful, even unto death. He was as one on whom the shadow of a vast, immeasurable trouble was beginning to fall darkly. He went forth to the garden of Gethsemane, as he had so often done before, for solitude and prayer. But now the weight of a great agony seemed to accumulate upon him. It overwhelmed him; till, his human strength failing, it pressed him to the ground. Then he, the Lord of angels, the eternal Son of the Father, needed and received the ministry

<small>He was like unto his brethren in his humanity.</small>

<small>He had a human dread of suffering.</small>

<small>Angels minister to him sinking under his agony.</small>

of angels. Ah! did not tears fall even from celestial eyes at the sight of his deep humiliation and distress?

Well may I linger here, and weep. Listen, O my soul! Behold thy Saviour kneeling alone beneath the ancient olive-trees! He offers up prayer and supplications, with strong crying and many tears, unto Him that is able to save him from death, and is heard in that he feared. Yes, *he feared!* — not death (for he was not saved from that), but lest his human strength and courage should prove unequal to his last great conflict. He *was* heard and answered in respect to this. Now he is comforted by the sympathy of the angelic messenger. Now the divine asserts itself in his consciousness again. Though he prays again and again that the cup may

<small>It is good to watch with him.</small>

<small>Heb. 5 : 7.</small>

pass from him, if this be possible, yet he is enabled to say, as expressive of his profoundest wish, "Nevertheless, not my will, but thine, be done!" He will not shrink, but will tread the wine-press alone, and accomplish all that belongs to his work as the world's Redeemer. What sublime self-sacrifice! What an unfathomable mystery of suffering! Let the sight of my blessed Lord, fainting and sinking to the earth with anguish, and, as it were, buried beneath huge billows of distress — all willingly endured for a guilty world, endured for me a sinner — penetrate my soul with deepest tenderness and grief!

<small>Matt. 26: 39, 42, 44.</small>

<small>Tenderness and grief in view of the Saviour's anguish.</small>

Most heartily would I lament, dear Lord, my many offenses for which it was needful that thou shouldst suffer. Most tenderly do

I recall thy tears and sorrows, that, fixing my thoughts on these, I may gain a just impression of the vastness of the debt of gratitude and love I owe. The world, while I come in contact with its trifles, and feel its earthly influences around me, would steal away the fervor of my affections. It would impair the energy of my faith and hope, repress my heavenward aspirations, and make me forgetful of the truth which I should ever keep in mind, that I am not my own, but thine. Often, I fear, it *has* beguiled me into listlessness and languor in respect to the holy duties of my great high calling; and imperceptibly, while I thought not of any danger, has chilled my Christian zeal, and made me too unmindful of thee, my faithful Redeemer, — too little anxious to maintain

<small>Contrition and gratitude.</small>

<small>Spirit of the world chilling.</small>

the glow and the consistency of a true devotion to thy service. But, in meditation on the scene through which thou didst pass in sorrowful Gethsemane, I would disarm it of its power, and renew the holy ardor of my soul. It is so that I would prepare my heart for a right participation in the sacramental feast. I shall think tearfully of the Garden while I remember thee.

GETHSEMANE.

SPREAD thick above, ye clouds, your dusky vail;
Hide from yon stars the Saviour's bitter woe:
Breathe, ye night winds, in murmurs sad and low;
Or lift, in fitful gusts, your mournful wail:
Listen, thou Olivet! and, Kedron's vale,
Catch the sad accents that are borne to thee
From yonder shade — thine own Gethsemane —
As when one pleadeth and doth not prevail.
See! to the earth the holy Sufferer sinks;
Weighs on his heart an anguish all unknown;
Bursts from his lips the thrice-repeated prayer,
Yet firm his will the utmost pang to bear;
Till for him, fainting while the cup he drinks,
Angels bring succors from the eternal throne!

"IN THE GARDEN WITH HIM."

WHERE climbs thy steep, fair Olivet,
    There is a spot most dear to me;
The spot with tears of sorrow wet,
    When Jesus knelt in agony.

I love in thought to linger there,
    To tread the hallowed ground alone,
Where, on the silent, midnight air,
    Rose heavenward, Lord, thy plaintive moan.

I fondly seek the olive shade
    That vailed thee when thy soul was wrung;
When angels came to bring thee aid,
    That oft to thee their harps had strung.

There, on the sacred turf, I kneel,
    And breathe my heart's deep love to thee,
While tender memories o'er me steal
    Of all thou didst endure for me.

Oh, mystery of anguish! when
    The Sinless felt sin's heavy woe!
Hell madly dreamed of triumph then,
    While thy dear head was bending low.

Vain dream! No grief shall evermore
    Stain, as with bloody sweat, thy brow:
Robed in all glory — thine before —
    The seraphim surround thee now.

Yet, Lord, from off the burning throne,
    Above yon stars that softly gleam,
Thou com'st to meet me here alone,
    By Kedron's old, familiar stream.

VII. CALVARY.

SABBATH MORNING.

THERE they crucified him! Yes, there at Jerusalem, the Holy City, the seat of the national religion, they who, as the chosen seed, and heirs of the promises, should have been the first to welcome the Son and Lord of David, delivered HIM who was the anointed King of Israel, the Messiah of the ages, to a shameful and cruel death! Amazing spiritual blindness, and desperate persistency in sin! Yet so the Scriptures

_{Luke 23: 33. His own nation reject and crucify the Messiah.}

_{Mark 14: 61, 62. Matt. 27: 11.}

were fulfilled, and a ruined world redeemed.

Luke 24: 25-27.

Christ, our Passover, was sacrificed for us. He gave himself for the life of the world. He once for all put away sin by the sacrifice of himself. Behold the Lamb of God, that taketh away the sin of the world! By his own blood he entered once into the holy place, having obtained eternal redemption for us. His blood is shed for many for the remission of sins. He is wounded for our transgressions; he is bruised for our iniquities. The Lord hath laid on him the iniquity of us all; and he bears our sins in his own body on the tree. This is indeed the Lamb slain from the foundation of the world in the counsels of Eternal Love,

1 Cor. 5:7.
John 6:51.
Heb. 9:26.
John 1:29.

Heb. 9:12.

Matt. 26:28.

Isaiah 53:5, 6.

1 Peter 2:24.

Rev. 13:8.

CALVARY.

and in the typical offering of slain victims unto God. He is lifted up upon the cross, like the brazen serpent in the wilderness, that the dying may look to him and live. _{John 3: 14, 15.}

> " See from his head, his hands, his feet,
> Sorrow and love flow mingled down·
> Did e'er such love and sorrow meet,
> Or thorns compose so rich a crown?"

For weary hours he hangs a bleeding victim, as if to fix the attention of the universe on the great atoning act which he performs. He dispenses mercy, even in the midst of his own sufferings, to one penitent and believing sinner. In the dreadful anguish — to us incomprehensible — of one forsaken, he cries out _{Luke 23: 43.} _{Matt. 27: 46, 50.}

once and again; and at last bows his head, saying, "It is finished!" and expires.

<small>John 19: 30.</small>

O Jesus! I sit down as if over against thy cross. I deliberately call to mind all that thou didst endure, and I see that in that great sacrifice of thine thou hast indeed opened a fountain for sin and for all uncleanness. Ah, now I perceive how deep the stain, how vast the ill-desert, of sin! Without the shedding of blood — of *thy* blood, O Most Holy! — there could be no remission. But thy blood cleanseth from all sin. As I behold thee lifted up upon the cross, thy body broken, the crimson streams issuing from thy wounds; as I listen to the cry wrung from thee in thine agony of spirit — the mys-

<small>Sitting over against the cross.</small>

<small>Zech. 13 1.</small>

<small>Sin seen in the light of the cross.</small>

<small>1 John 1·7.</small>

<small>Matt. 27: 46.</small>

tery of which agony I can not comprehend, since it involved the hiding of thy Father's face — I feel alike the infinite love and absolute justice of God, and the profoundest conviction that he can and will forgive and justify every sinner that believeth. Now I understand, O Jesus! thy touching words: "This is my body, which is given for you; my blood, which is shed for you." God's love and justice revealed in the death of Jesus. Rom. 3: 23-26. Luke 22: 19: 20.

My dearest Lord! on this thy most precious and all-availing sacrifice I rely in humble faith. On this sure foundation, laid by thee, I build my immortal hopes. All unworthy in myself, for thy sake I am forgiven, justified, have peace with God, and am received of him as a child. And what shall I say? How shall I pay the mighty debt I Faith relies on the sacrifice of Jesus. Rom. 5:1; 8:14.

owe? I thank thee; I praise thee. I would laud and magnify thy name for ever. Afresh, and most deliberately and heartily, I give myself, with all that I am and have, to thee. <small>Divine life in Christ, and full salvation.</small> Let me abide ever in vital union with thee, and live in thy life. Let love to thee be the ruling passion of my heart, the determining impulse of all the actions of my life. While I live, I would be wholly thine. When I come at last to die, may the assurance that thou art mine — my sufficient and ever-living Redeemer — dispel all darkness, and give me complete serenity and peace! Then, to the glory of thy grace, permit me to behold thy face in righteousness.

All these rich blessings, the purchase of thy death upon the cross, wilt thou seal to me, a humble believer, while I shall commune with thee at thy table in the remembrance of thy death. Let me so feed upon thy body and blood, that I may have the delightful consciousness of eternal life begun within my soul. Oh, blessed, blessed day, when that life shall be made perfect, and, with all the redeemed before the throne, I shall unite in saying —

<small>All good in Christ sealed to the believer at his table.</small>

WORTHY IS THE LAMB THAT WAS SLAIN, AND HAS REDEEMED US TO GOD BY HIS BLOOD!

THE SACRIFICE.

WONDER of wonders! on the cross he dies!
Man of the ages — David's mighty Son —
The eternal Word, who spake and it was done,
What time, of old, he formed the earth and skies.
Abashed be all the wisdom of the wise!
Let the wide earth through all her kingdoms know
The promised Lamb of God, whose blood should flow,
For human guilt the grand, sole sacrifice.
No more need altar smoke, nor victim bleed:
'Tis finished! — the great mystery of love.
Ye sin-condemned, by this blood 'tis decreed
Ye stand absolved; behold the curse remove!
O Christ! thy deadly wounds, thy mortal strife,
Crush death and hell, and give immortal life!

VIA DOLOROSA.

I SEE my Lord, the pure, the meek, the lowly.
    Along the mournful way in sadness tread!
The thorns are on his brow; and he, the Holy,
    Bearing his cross, to Calvary is led.

Silent he moveth on, all uncomplaining,
    Though wearily his grief and burden press;
And foes, nor shame nor pity now restraining,
    With scoff and jeering, mock his deep distress.

'Tis hell's dark hour; yet calm, himself resigning,
    Even as a lamb that goeth to be slain,
The wine-press lone he treadeth, unrepining,
    And falling blood-drops all his raiment stain.

In mortal weakness 'neath his burden sinking,
    The Son of God accepts a mortal's aid!
Then passes on to Golgotha, unshrinking,
    Where love's divinest sacrifice is made.

Dear Lord! what though my path be set with sorrow,
  And oft beneath some heavy cross I groan?
My soul, weighed down, shall strength and courage borrow
  At thought of harder griefs which thou hast known.

And I in tears will yet look up with gladness,
  And hope when troubles most my hope would drown:
The mournful way which thou didst pass in sadness
  Was but the way to GLORY and thy CROWN!

AT THE TABLE.

LET the thought that Jesus, unseen, is with you, completely possess your mind when seated at the table. Be collected, reverent, and tender in spirit. *Jesus present though unseen.* Let not a sense of your unworthiness make you afraid, but remember that this is a feast of love, instituted expressly for penitent sinners. Reflect that the mere outward receiving of the bread and of the wine can of itself convey to you no blessing. It is only as it assists your faith to apprehend the Saviour in the great act of making his atoning sacrifice; it is only as you inwardly *The bread and wine appointed as aids to faith.* receive him as, through his death, your all-sufficient Redeemer, and feed on him as the Bread of Life — that the elements presented in the Supper fulfill to you their end. While, therefore, the ordinance proceeds, let your mind and heart be occupied with such exercises as the following: —

I.

Recognition of Christ as present. Lord Jesus! thou art here to meet and bless me at thy table. I am thine. I trust thee, love thee, adore thee. Reveal thyself more fully to my soul. Impart unto me the Holy Ghost, that by his aid my spirit may be quickened, warmed, and purified, and brought into a holy sympathy with thee.

II.

"This is my body!" Yes, dearest Lord! I see in the broken bread a lively emblem of

AT THE TABLE.

that body broken for sin — pierced, bleeding, dying, on the bitter cross. I behold the Lamb of God slain — the one sufficient sacrifice for sin. I hate my own sins, that helped to plat that crown of thorns, and to drive those cruel nails. "Broken for you!" O Jesus! it was indeed for me. By thy cross, even I may become — have become, I humbly hope — a child of the living God.

Faith in the dying Lamb.

III.

As I take this symbol, O thou Bread of Life! I would spiritually feed on thee. I open my heart to receive thee; I give myself to thee anew; I seal my covenant-vows anew; I take thee anew to be my Saviour and my Lord. In this act of eating the sacramental bread, I

Christ received as the Bread of Life.

feel my soul united to thee, and receive of thy life and strength. Lovingly and trust-ingly, O my Beloved! I look up into thy blessed face, and thy smile falls like sunshine on my heart. May I abide ever in thy love!

The unity of love.

IV.

And now, with a heart melting into thankful tenderness, let me receive the cup. "This is my blood!" Yes, O my soul! this only can wash away thy sins, and make thee pure in the sight of the All-holy. This cleanseth from all sin. Apply to me afresh, thou who art at once the Sacrifice of atonement and the great High Priest, thy most precious blood. As I taste the wine in affectionate remembrance of thy bloody death, I

The cup gratefully received,

with new faith in the atonement.

lay myself again as if beneath thy cross, and entreat thee to grant me the assurance of peace with God.

V.

In this receiving of the bread and wine, I would not forget, dear Lord, that I have fellowship not only with thee, but with my fellow-disciples. In them thou wilt have me recognize my brethren, and love even the humblest and the most imperfect of them for thy sake. I feel my heart warm towards them, as members with thee of thy body. Help me to be tender in spirit, patient, helpful, and forgiving, in all my intercourse with such as bear thy name. Make me more watchful to fulfill the new commandment.

The communion of saints.

Love to the Christian household.

VI.

Christ's perpetual presence sought. Though I must now leave thy table, O Jesus! let me not, Lord, leave thy presence. Make thine abode in my unworthy heart. In the dark hours of temptation and trouble, in the moments when sadness and despondency oppress me, and especially when the hour of death approaches, may I hear thy comforting voice, and know that thou rememberest me as I have endeavored to remember thee this day!

Remarks. It is by such meditations and petitions that the devout disciple will enter into the spirit of the Holy Supper, and make his own the benefits it was intended to convey. These are, of course, given merely as examples, illustrative of the real nature of the ordinance. They are designed to express the substance of the exercises — more or less extended and diversified, as the case may be — with which each one at the table should occupy his mind and heart.

AFTER THE SACRAMENT.

SABBATH EVENING.

IT is the close of the Sabbath; and it has indeed been a sabbath to my soul. I have been permitted to sit with Christ and with his friends, as in heavenly places; and the affecting fact that I am not my own, but have been bought with a price, has once more been distinctly placed before me. Have I not met my Lord indeed? Has he not smiled upon my soul, and whispered in its deep recesses the assurance that I am his? Has he not breathed upon me, and said, "Receive thou the Holy Ghost"? It must be so, if I have rightly partaken of the feast.

After the Sacrament.

What then? Henceforth it must be my care to live, not unto myself, but unto Him who died for me, and rose again. This I resolve to-night, that by his grace it shall be. Yes, O my loving Redeemer! who now ever livest Head over all things for thy Church, I am earnestly determined that in thy strength I will every day be an example unto the believers, and a light in this dark world. To-night, therefore, I beseech thee, help me to gird up my loins anew, and to set forward with redoubled zeal and diligence in the way of Christian duty. Assist me, with watchfulness and prayer, with Christian prudence and self-denial, to keep myself unspotted from the world. Let me find it in my heart to visit the fatherless and widows in their affliction, and to go about doing good, after the example of my Lord. Especially aid me,

O my Saviour! to overcome temptation, to amend my faults of character, and to triumph entirely over the sins that most easily beset me. Give me the calmness of self-control, patience under trials, and submission to all thy will. Make me, finally, strong in the Lord and in the power of his might, firm and steadfast in Christian principle, and ever faithful to truth and to thy cause, till my work of life is done.

Lord, what wilt thou have me to do? Make me to run in the way of thy commandments. Let me be able to say at last, in thine own emphatic words, "I HAVE GLORIFIED THEE ON THE EARTH; I HAVE FINISHED THE WORK WHICH THOU GAVEST ME TO DO." All this I ask through thy dear cross and passion. Amen.

DELIGHT IN CHRIST.

ESUS, thou Joy of loving hearts,
  Thou Fount of life, thou Light of men,
From the best bliss that earth imparts
  We turn unfilled to thee again.

Thy truth unchanged hath ever stood;
  Thou savest those that on thee call:
To them that seek thee thou art good;
  To them that find thee, all in all!

We taste thee, O thou living Bread,
  And long to feed upon thee still;
We drink of thee, the Fountain-head,
  And thirst our souls from thee to fill.

Our restless spirits yearn for thee
    Where'er our changeful lot is cast;
Glad when thy gracious smile we see,
    Blest when our faith can hold thee fast.

O Jesus! ever with us stay;
    Make all our moments calm and bright;
Chase the dark night of sin away;
    Shed o'er the world thy holy light.

FAITH.

MY Faith looks up to thee,
Thou Lamb of Calvary,
   Saviour divine!
Now hear me while I pray:
Take all my guilt away;
O let me, from this day,
   Be wholly thine.

May thy rich grace impart
Strength to my fainting heart,
   My zeal inspire!
As thou hast died for me,
O may my love to thee
Pure, warm, and changeless be —
   A living fire!

While life's dark maze I tread,
And griefs around me spread,
   Be thou my guide;

Bid darkness turn to day,
Wipe sorrow's tears away,
Nor let me ever stray
    From thee aside.

When ends life's transient dream,
When death's cold, sullen stream
    Shall o'er me roll —
Blest Saviour! then, in love,
Fear and distrust remove;
O bear me safe above —
    A ransomed soul!

www.ingramcontent.com/pod-product-compliance
Lightning Source LLC
Chambersburg PA
CBHW030411170426
43202CB00010B/1563